Shields of Men
Our Lives for Yours

by The Four Menards

SHIELDS OF MEN: OUR LIVES FOR YOURS

www.Twitter.com/TheFourMenards

Illustrations by Lucas Frazier;

Book Design by Darlene Swanson.

Cover by Adrienne Menard, design by Darlene Swanson.

Printed in the United States of America

ISBN   978-0-9887969-0-4 (paperback)
978-0-9887969-1-1 (hard cover)

We dedicate this book to all of those who
have given their lives, "so that others may live!"

Our daily thoughts and prayers are with them and
their own loved ones, who supported them
in their endeavor to serve and
come to the aid of those in need.

God bless you.

We would also like to dedicate this book to
Chief John Henry Jamason.
Our uncle, our role model, and our friend.

We love you, Uncle Jim!

Contents

THE TATTERED BADGE

I rushed to get the kids to school and be at work on time,
The blue lights flashed, as though they meant
to solve some vicious crime!

The smug policeman sauntered over, adding to the stress;
I asked if he must cite me, and he answered coldly, "Yes."

I felt the urge to punch his face; I wished him greatest harm;
I snatched the ticket from his hand and hoped I'd break his arm;
"Oh come down off your great high horse, you macho man," I said.
He didn't hear me, which was good; I added, "Go drop dead!"

The office gang all understood, with stories of their own,
"That's why the escalated hatred for those pigs has grown!"

Our manager continued laughing, "Look at all the names,
Like 'bears', and 'fuzz', and 'county mounties', from their little games!"

"That's right," another worker added, "they just drive around,
And flash their sickening little lights at every error found;

They don't concern themselves at all with hardships they inflict,
And wallow in their speed traps with amusement when we're tricked!"

I felt much better after venting, "One more bill to pay!
I wanted to ask that smug swine what good he does each day!

Our taxes give this fool a badge to puff up and show off;
We're probably even paying for the donuts in his trough!"

"I heard that," laughed the gentleman, who brings our daily mail,
"When I'm not in my work truck, they are heavy on my trail!

Say, which cop was it, anyway?" He headed for the door,
"Oh, precious little Theodore! Ted Scroggs- who stands six-four!

He couldn't let this matter slide! Oh no, he is too great!
Why, he's the meanest, leanest pig in this pathetic state!

I hope his wife is cheating, and his kids wind up on drugs;
These cops are here to bully everyone, like high school thugs!"

The mailman waved goodbye and laughed, "I've had more than my share,
Of nonsense from that Teddy Scroggs; each time I speed – he's there!

And never cuts the slightest break for folks just on the run;
'Oh no,' he says, 'Your nonsense, sir, could kill somebody's son!'"

"Well good for him, the safety king, just knocked my budget out;
I've no idea where this will come from, or what to take out!

I wonder how he'd like it if his family was harassed;
His wife and kids are all immune!" I thought out loud, aghast.

I scraped my budget for that month; watched every dime I spent,
But also watched my speed each day, no matter where I went!

I finally came to peace with things and settled back to see,
My life go on, and I might add, quite uneventfully.

Months later, settled at my desk, my coffee cup in place,
Our manager burst in and shouted – panic in his face:

"There are three gunmen at the school, they're making no demands,
They'll take no bargains," he continued, laptop in his hands.

"My God!" I lost my vision and my hearing at this thought,
I couldn't move- I was stunned still, from fear the message brought.

"I'm going down there, now!" I screamed. My boss said, "It is blocked!"
The other girls around me couldn't speak – they were so shocked.

We pulled into the school yard, as close as we were allowed;
And tried to keep our sanity, among the roaring crowd.

The officers were very kind but kept the group controlled,
I heard one say, "My son is in there too," as he patrolled.

We heard some gunshots as we prayed and waited for reports;
From where we were, I saw the medics with police escorts.

The loud speaker announcement blared – "The gunmen are all dead."
And parents waited anxiously for what they finally said … ….

"The students are all safe, although one boy is still in shock;
A target for one gunman, he was fortunately blocked.

The officer who saved him is in very dangerous states,
We won't release the name yet, as his fear-filled family waits."

They called my name, and I went forward, guided by a cop,
"Ma'am, just keep moving right up toward the ambulance, then stop.

They need to take your boy in, for he was a target here;
His health's determined stable, though, so lay aside your fear."

I reached the front and saw my son, as tears streamed down my cheek;
Although I tried to thank the Lord, I could not even speak.

My little son looked smaller on that stretcher being sent,
To our local hospital, I held him as we went.

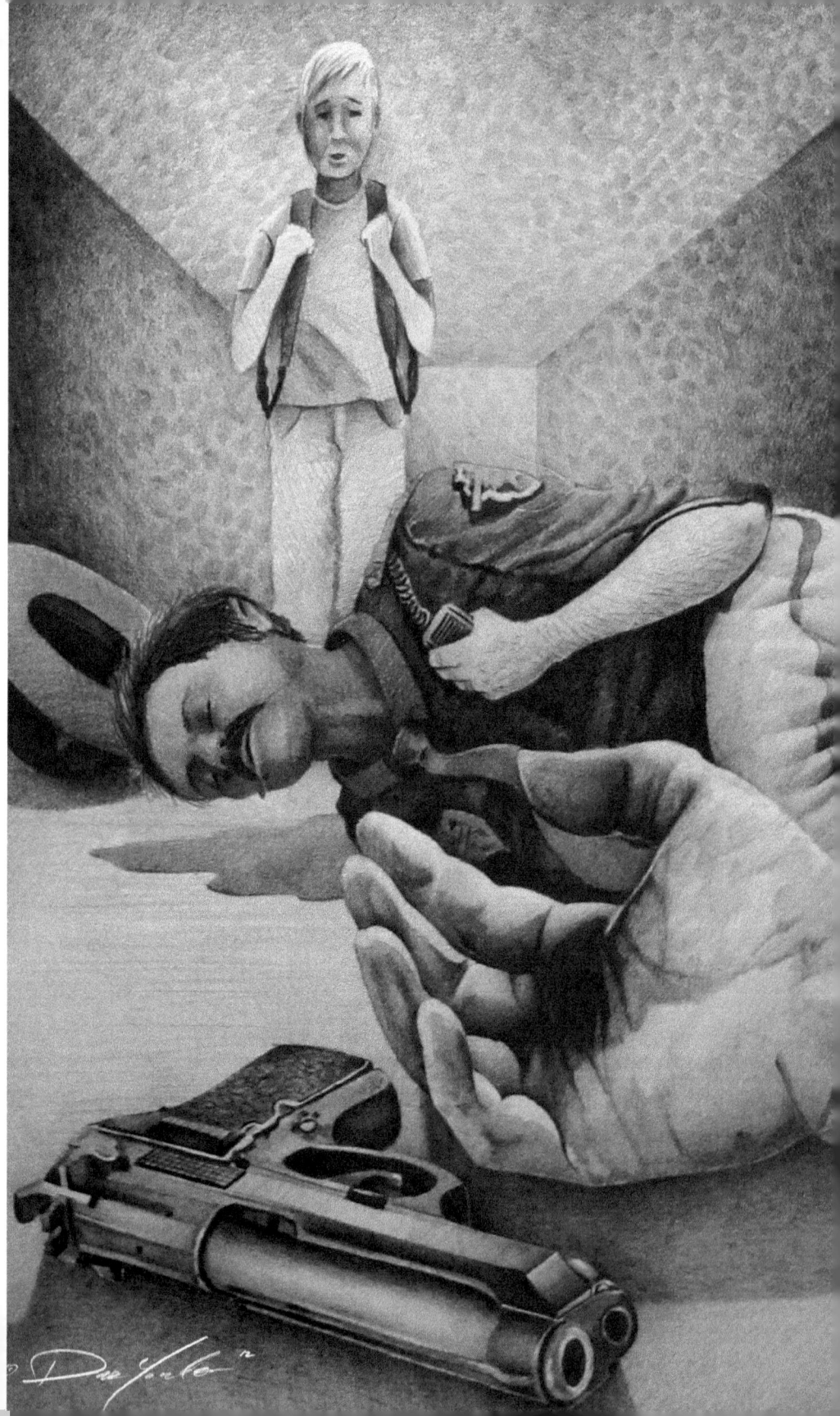

The ER was the typical, chaotic blast of dread,
"Here comes the cop who saved that kid," the news reporter said.

"They don't think that he'll make it," a policeman spoke in tears,
"His wife and kids have just pulled up, to face their greatest fears!"

My son recovered quickly and relayed the story well,
"The only gunman still alive, came toward me, I could tell,

A real tall cop jumped in my path and shot the gunman dead,
But just before he saved me, he was hit by him, instead."

The little boy continued, "His blood poured down on the floor;
Next thing I knew, the paramedics showed up at the door.

The cop insisted that they take me first; I couldn't talk,
And then they carried me outside – because I couldn't walk."

Behind the curtain, more policemen shouted, "It was Ted!"
I heard his sobbing wife and children asking, "Is he dead?"

"No. No, he isn't, honey, but it doesn't look too good."
"My God," I prayed, "please help this man; please save him if You would!"

I knelt beside my little son, and sobbed as I prayed for,
This officer who saved my son; I'd sneered at weeks before.

I heard his own boy tell the press, "I hope my dad's okay;
He is a superhero, and he saves lives every day!

We need him to come home with us, for he's too young to die,
And we can't live without him, Sir, we wouldn't want to try!

I watched him suit up for his job today; he wore his vest,
Then took his gun, and cuffs, and tear gas; carrying the rest.

He grinned at me and said, 'You help your mom for me today;
When I come home from work, we're going to the park to play.'"

This child's mom was so upset she couldn't speak at all;
But waited with the others on the force, out in the hall.

I thought of all the things I'd said about the man upstairs,
The surgeons fighting for his life and I, with all my prayers.

My own son rested quietly and waited for release,
While halls and waiting rooms continued to fill with police.

And as I knelt there, I remembered many other stops,
When I was treated very nicely by the city cops.

I laughed while I was crying, when I thought about the day,
That I had missed my exit, and backed up to find my way!

The officer who stopped me asked if I knew what I'd done,
And added that the violation was a high-point one.

He shook his head in disbelief, and made the traffic wait,
Then helped me exit safely, from that busy interstate.

I never will forget his struggle, trying not to smile,
And how concerned he was for us the whole tenth of a mile;

How I had prayed for safety in his work, right there and then,
I still could hear his gentle warning, "Don't do this again."

The hours seemed like months now, but we finally got the word,
"It looks like Teddy could pull through!" is what we overheard.

"It will take months of therapy before he walks again,
But let's keep praying for his life; we need to give blood, men!"

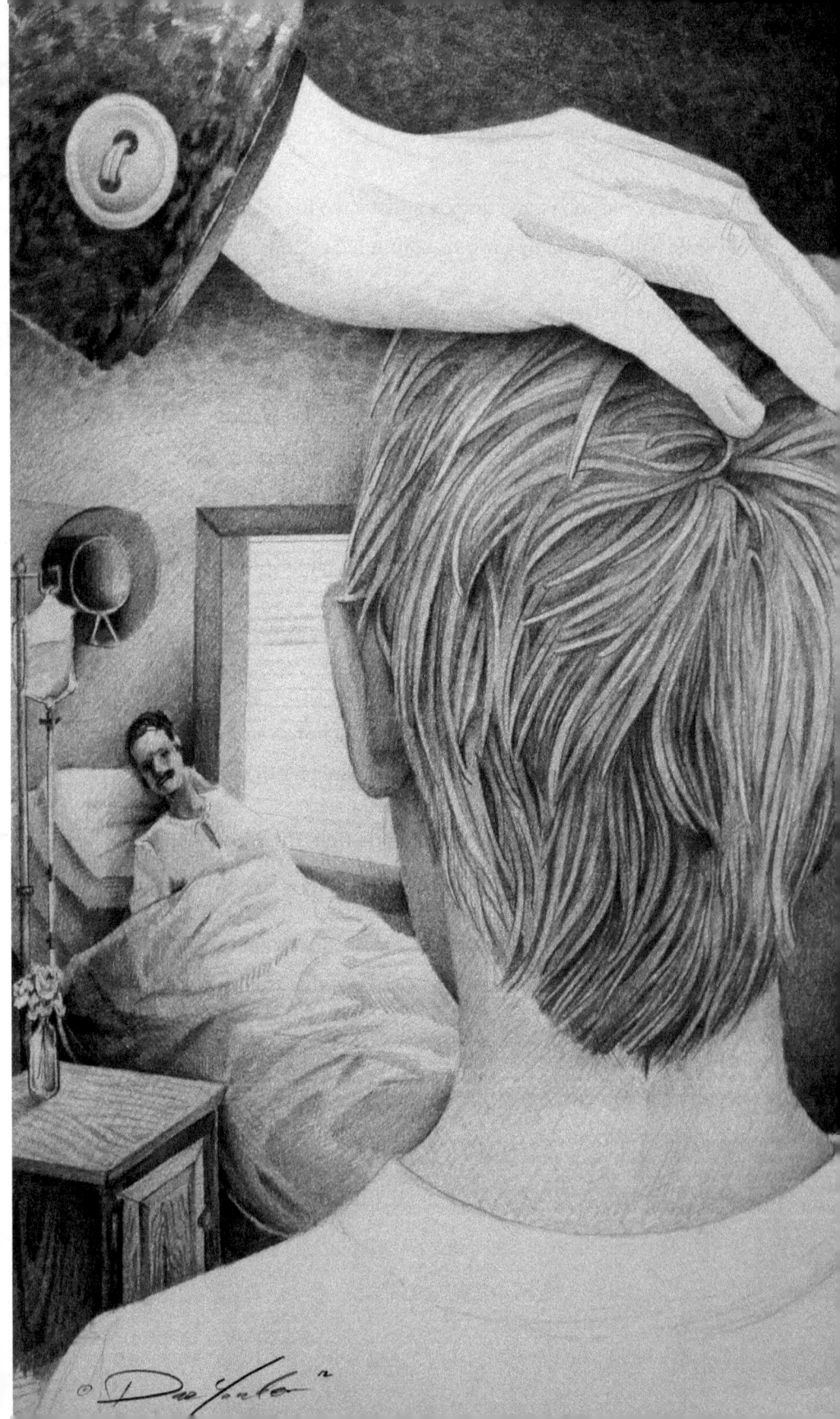

A few days later, my son asked to go and visit Ted;
He wanted to say thank you, so, "Of course we will!" I said.

I couldn't raise my eyes to meet the hero in that chair;
My son had made a gift for him, with hours of childlike care.

"You saved my life, Sir," my son said, "without you, I'd be dead!
I want to pay you back somehow," and this is what Scroggs said,

"Do well in school, and never speed," he smiled, "and we'll be square."
Ted took the gift, with loving pride, then tousled my son's hair.

"And, Mom," he added, "Do look up and know that what was done,
Was in my line of duty, Ma'am — God saved your little son.

So don't feel badly for me now, or anything that's passed."
"I am so grateful, Officer," I said in tears, at last.

– The Four Menards

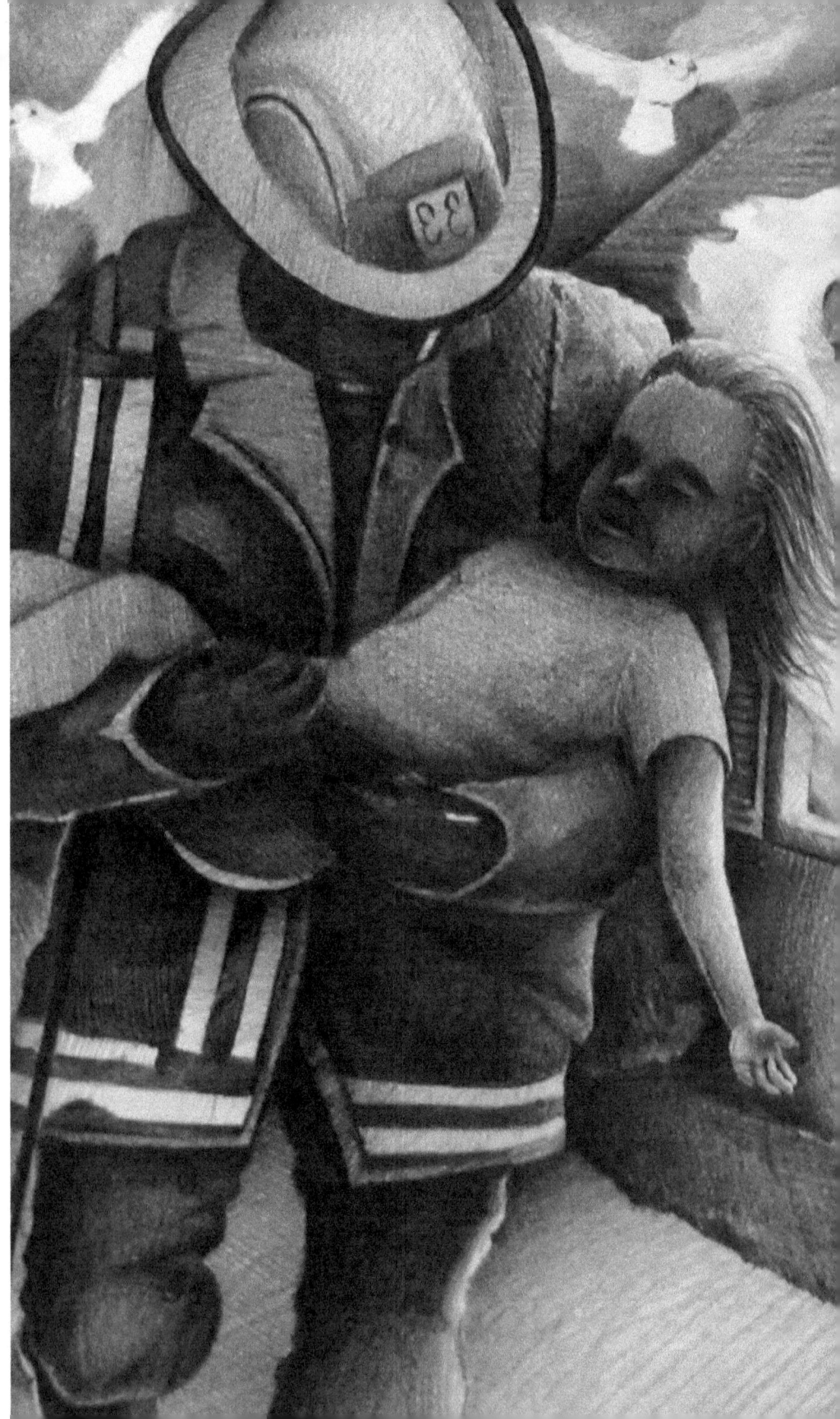

FIGHTING FIRE
WITH ANGELS

The setting is engulfed in smoke,
And panic fills the air;
The sounds of screaming, frightened cries,
Outweigh the sirens' blare.

Among the great confusion there,
The firefighters stand;
Prepared to risk their very lives,
To do the task at hand.

Their thoughts are with endangered souls;
Their boundless courage drives,
These fearless heroes forward now,
To save the victims' lives.

With no thought for themselves, they run,
Through danger, toward the calls,
From wounded and from compromised,
Within the blazing walls.

Each rescued person their reward,
They carry out the plan;
But sometimes, Someone higher up,
Calls home His "fallen-man."

Although we cannot see Him there,
God's in that building too.
He hears each prayer that's sent to Him;
And sees His children through.

The fallen-man He chose today,
Left in His mighty arms;
Although his mortal body lay,
Among the stilled alarms.

What of new fires yet to come?
This hero will return;
Among the team of angels sent,
Wherever buildings burn.

And when his comrades feel him there,
They will recall this day;
And understand the strength they bear,
Because he's sent their way.

He gave his life to help someone,
Then smiled – which isn't odd;
This angel died the way he lived,
And touched the face of God!

– The Four Menards

In loving memory of Captain Jeffrey Bowen and all firefighters
who have been called from the line of duty to engage in the
Ultimate Task Force, led by the Greatest Protector of All.

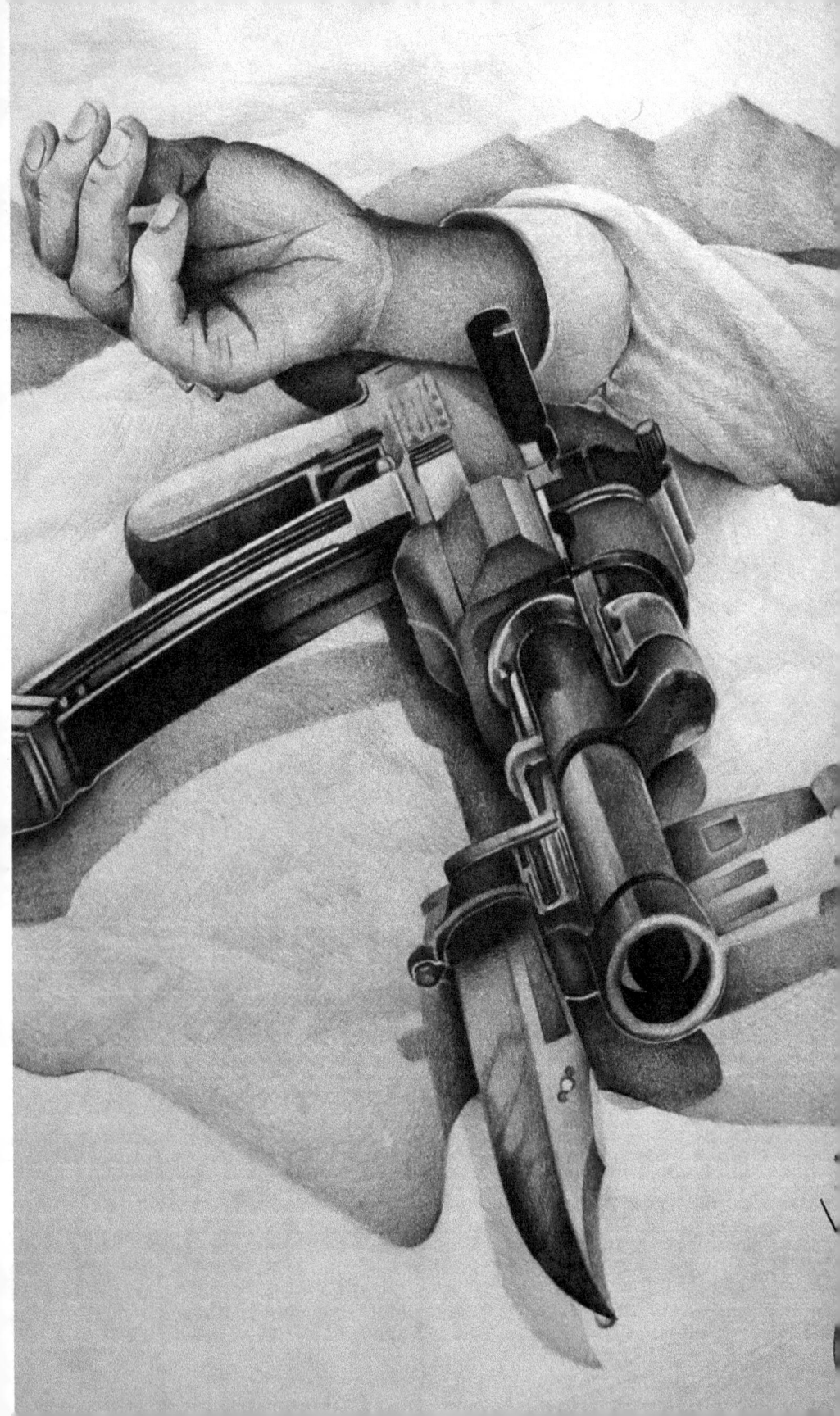

THE OCEAN'S GREATEST TALE

God looked down from the sapphire sky, upon His roaring sea;
He shook His head and gave a sigh, and said, "How can this be?
That such a neatly contained world can be so unaware,
Of what goes on across the seas, in that great place they share!"

"What is it, Lord?" an angel asked, proceeding to His side,
"Do You see something we must dread, amid the changing tide?"
"Ah, yes," the Mighty Father's nod gave cause to scan the scene,
Of ocean shores and all the people living in between.

"Well, come here closer by My side, and stand right next to Me;
You take that shore, I'll take this – We'll call out what We see."
"A brightly colored pail for sand – a castle building set!"
"A stray canteen, some floating tags, a bloody bayonet."

"A cooler filled with summer treats, and different things to drink!"
"A soldier crawling on the shore – afraid to even blink."
"A musical device of sorts – and dancing girls and boys!"
"A set of blood-caked earplugs to survive the blasting noise."

"Hey, check this out- a colored float that holds a group of four!"
"A man's been shot – he's praying that he'll see his wife once more."
"A grown up frowns; the beer is gone, 'Oh what could be more grim?'"
"A comrade offered his canteen – so nothing's left for him."

"Great sandwiches of many kinds, fried chicken, and some chips!"
"A soldier's wiping sweat that burns the skin of his chapped lips."
"Say! – Neat containers for the food with special air-tight seals!"
"This group of soldiers had no sleep, and certainly no meals."

"The seagulls fill a peaceful sky, and dive for scraps of bread!"
"The sky here - clogged with blackened smoke and war planes overhead."
"A mother putting sunscreen on her child in shoreline foam!"
"Another fallen soldier, who will never go back home."

"The people here are filled with cheer, as children laugh and play!"
"The soldiers on My beach just hope they'll see another day."
"Some children running with their pails, collecting shells galore!"
"The sand on My side's caked with blood, and shrapnel lines the shore."

The Father nodded once again, and motioned toward the beach;
"How many people realize the relationship of each?"
"And what of that among the homelands far beyond the shore?"
The angel asked, observing all the side effects of war.

"Where some folks have a nice safe home, a business, and free speech,
But others die so cruelly for the things they say or teach?"
"The freedom and the carefree way with which some lives are styled,
Was gifted to them by the acts of someone else's child!"

Those soldiers fighting for our lives upon the same huge turf,
Had thoughts of their own families playing in that same grand surf!
So every time you see a veteran, give him a salute;
For every gun and helmet and for each canteen and boot,

That found its way to battlefields, from sea to endless sea,
To keep a grand America, that's safe for you and me!
And every time we think about our ocean's sparkling foam,
Say twice the prayers for those from there, who never did come home.

– The Four Menards

God bless all of you who gave your time and lives for us!

THE LAST RESORT

We revved the engines on our bikes and took off for the ride;
The sky was blue, the sun was out, where did this downpour hide?
We pulled aside to safety to wait out the raging storm,
And tossed our helmets and our jackets off - they were too warm.

Now underneath the overpass, we both opened a beer,
An older dude pulled in by us and laughed, "It's dry in here."
As we observed the blackened sky, we chatted with the dude,
Sure, he was old- but cool, and had a laid back attitude.

This older man who'd parked by us now dismounted his bike;
My friend laughed, "Clear skies make me ask myself what Heaven's like.
A bunch of goodie two-shoes - all the soap box fools we know –
And choirs of shrieking angels! Heck – I wouldn't want to go!"

He stretched and lit a cigarette, while trying to conceal,
The beer he held, then glanced my way, "Do you think Heaven's real?"
I looked up at the sky but didn't answer right away;
I didn't know this other guy, or what I ought to say.

"Heck, I don't know what to believe; the world's a mess today;
I'm not sure that I'd qualify if Heaven came my way!"

The older man was listening, but didn't say a word;
"Hey dude," my friend joked, "you have been around, what have you heard?"

"Well now, let's see," he scratched his head, a twinkle in his eye,
"I'm not sure how to tell you, but I'll give it my best try!

Some think it's just a holy spot where angels sing and pray,
And others say that it's a giant party every day.

But me, I think the best description is unending bliss;
From what I know, it's sure a blast I wouldn't want to miss."

My friend and I got comfortable and hoped to hear some more;
The guy spoke softly, but we heard amidst the traffic roar.

He realized we were waiting and unwrapped a piece of gum;
Then nodded toward us as he asked if we would care for some.

"I think that Heaven would be close to a vacation land,
But not just any," he continued, holding up his hand.

"The perfect trip – the nicest time that you have ever had –
Where everything was wonderful and nothing there was bad;
Or if you never had that chance, then I'll put it this way:
I think that Heaven is a place you'd always want to stay."

"So you think that it's a resort, with fun and drinks and food,
And everything is perfect there, and no one's ever rude?"

I waited for his answer but my friend sneered, "That's a hoot!"
The man was calmly pressing water from his riding boot.

My friend continued chanting – "Gorgeous seas, an awesome shore,
And 'purple mountains majesty?'" Dude nodded, "That and more."

I didn't like the taunting from my friend, this guy was cool;
But he was still antagonizing - acting like a fool.

"So you just run along and hope to see this golden gate?"
"Ah, there are no deterrents, son; there is no war, no hate;

And everyone is filled with joy because they're filled with love."
"Oh sure! There are no class distinctions in that land above?"

"The residents are awesome there, son, everyone you meet,
Is marvelous! Remarkable – folks hugging in the street;
You'd love them, for they'd all love you- just for the man you are,
Because each cherished single soul there is a super star!"

"But what of people that we hate?" I laughed, "The jerks from here?"
He smiled back, "They won't be jerks – those feelings disappear.
They wouldn't be the same in Heaven, and neither would you;
You'd mutually be filled with peace - a thrill you never knew.

Did someone ever cross your path and you felt warm inside;
An unexpected kindness where your joy was hard to hide?
Or any touching goodness that you wanted to repay?
Those, multiplied a million times, each second of each day!

No need for competition there - no jealousy or greed,
There's everything you'd hope for – there's no sadness and no need."
My friend sneered, "You believe in God! Would He bring up my bike?"
The old man smiled and crossed his arms, "I'm sure, son, if you'd like."

"So you are saying anything we want – that's quite a task,
I don't believe you think that's true!" Dude nodded, "You did ask."
My friend kept shouting, "WATERFALLS – or snow just on a whim,
In case you want to ski, or did you say you'd rather swim?"

The old dude leaned against the wall with interest as he heard,
Sarcastic mocking sentences, that housed each bitter word.
"So animals of every kind all calm enough to kiss?"
"Ah, yes, perhaps a long lost dog you really loved and miss,"

Dude kept responding pleasantly, no anger in his voice,
"You can believe or you may not; it's every man's own choice."
"Oh yeah, I get it, man, that's what the Sunday schools all teach."
"I hope they're adding that this promise is within your reach.

For Heaven is available to everyone, you know,
Your ticket to get in there, son, is just to want to go."
My friend looked up and said, "I blew my chances but, hey, thanks;
From nasty things I've done today to early childhood pranks."

"Oh, I don't know," the old man laughed and started toward his bike,
"I wouldn't sweat the small stuff, son, but you do what you like,"
Then raised his eyebrows in an entertaining reprimand;
"Oh well, dude, no offense," my friend got up and shook his hand.

"I just don't want to think of dying, you know what I mean?
It isn't easy to believe in things we've never seen."
"Son, having faith in what's to come are choices you must make,
But living with a fear that death's the end, is a mistake."

He pointed to our beers with that same twinkle in his eye,
"And, 'dudes,' that's not the drink for riders who don't want to die."
The storm was gone, the sun was out, and yet we sat in place,
For something moved us, just the look of peace on this man's face.

He waved and rode his bike away, but left us in deep thought;
We tapped our drinks together with the lesson we'd been taught.
But neither of us really wanted to take off just yet,
Somehow we knew this was a day we never would forget.

We swallowed our last sips of beer, and jolted with a shock!
The drinks were quite amazing, but a very different stock.
The cans were full and icy cold with label changes made;
"A Beverage From The Last Resort – Dude's Frosty Lemonade."

I stood exclaiming, "Hey, there *is* an endless life to come!"
My friend was laughing through his tears, "My cigarettes are gum!
I love that Dude," my friend cried, "and although it may seem odd,
Might I suggest that we begin addressing Him as God?"

– *The Four Menards*

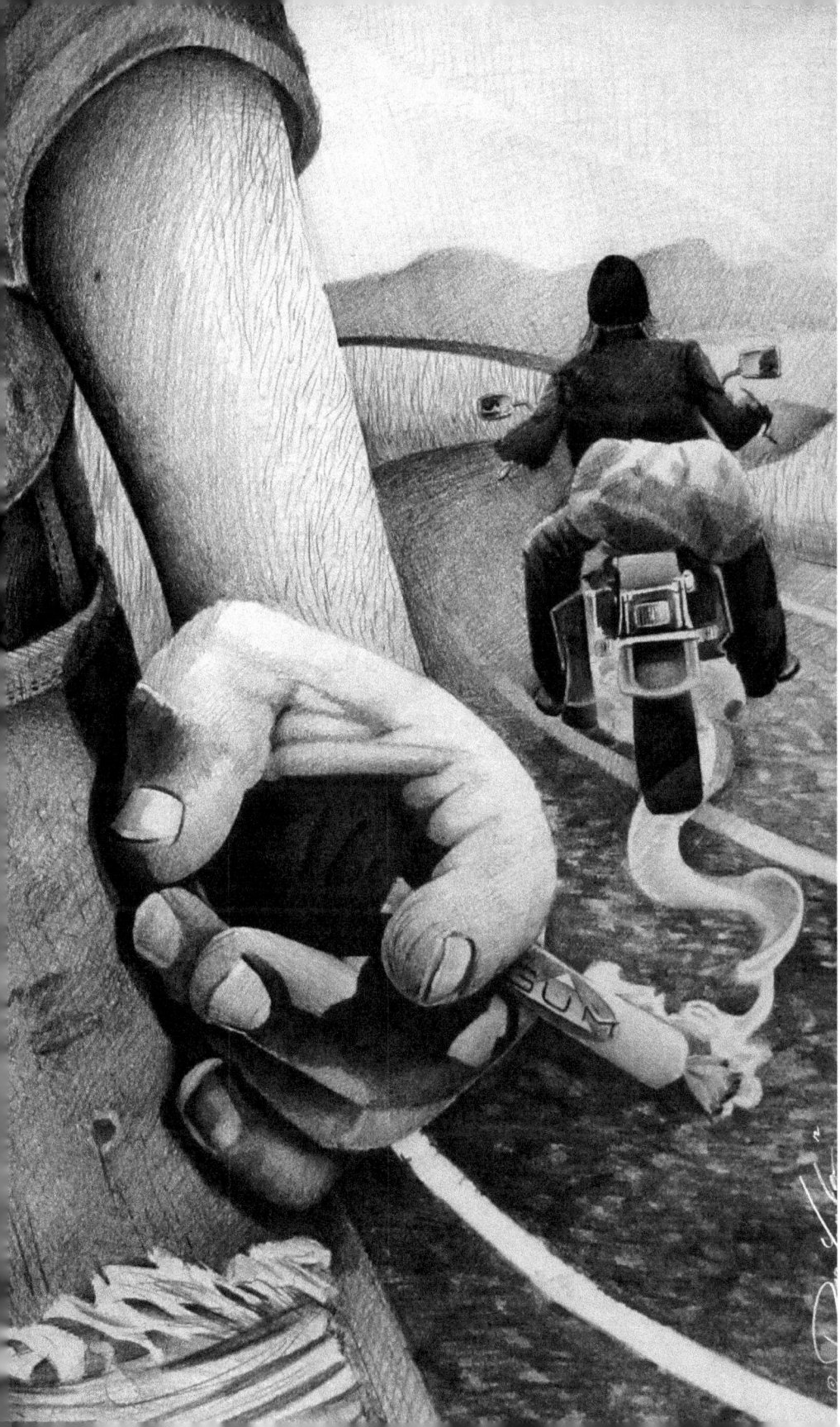

Also by The Four Menards:

So Say We All – "B" Is For Bravery

The First Mrs. Solberg (series)

Anybody Want A Peanut?

The Canopy House (children's series)

The Top of the Bottom (children's series)

The Cherub in the Lily Field

Wood, You Be Real!

The Moon Means Business!

Who Do I Think You Are?

Cardinal Christmas

The Four Menards are a family based in Asheville,
North Carolina. They write colorful children's books
in verse with entertaining, strong, moral messages.

www.ingramcontent.com/pod-product-compliance
Lightning Source LLC
Chambersburg PA
CBHW071940020426
42331CB00010B/2953